core belief

Bible Study Series
for junior high/middle school

contents:

the Core Belief: ▼Evil

If Satan wants us to ignore one Core Christian Belief, this is it. Satan wants you and your kids to remain uninformed about him and his realm.

Granted, we all have our own evil sides to deal with. After all, when Adam and Eve tasted that forbidden fruit, they doomed all of us to inherit a morally evil nature. And along with moral evil came natural evil—those disasters that strike and create damage and death. We have only ourselves to blame.

Yet while we're all responsible for our own sin, Satan loves to lead us to it.

But God's still in control. He has limited the amount of havoc Satan can wreak on creation. In the end, good will win over evil, and those who've accepted Jesus will have no more death, mourning, crying, or pain.

Isn't that good news for today's young people to hear?

the ▼Helpful Stuff

the ▼Studies

core belief™

Bible Study Series
for junior high/middle school

THE TRUTH
ABOUT
Evil

Loveland, Colorado

The Truth About Evil

Core Belief Bible Study Series

Copyright © 1998 Group Publishing, Inc.

Credits

Editor: Jim Hawley
Creative Development Editor: Karl Leuthauser
Chief Creative Officer: Joani Schultz
Copy Editor: Patti Leach
Art Director: Ray Tollison
Cover Art Director: Jeff A. Storm
Computer Graphic Artist/Illustrator: Eris Klein
Photographer: Jafe Parsons
Production Manager: Peggy Naylor

ISBN 0-7644-0854-2

10 9 8 7 6 5 4 3 2 1   07 06 05 04 03 02 01 00 99 98

Printed in the United States of America.

▼Evil
as a Core Christian Belief

You probably don't need to convince your kids that evil exists. They face it every day at home, in school, and on the streets. Sometimes evil tempts them. Sometimes evil torments them. No matter what they do or where they go, evil always lurks nearby.

Since your young people can't escape evil, they need to know how to overcome it in their lives. The studies within this Core Christian Belief can prepare your kids for battle by helping them think biblically about the origin and nature of evil. When they recognize that sin and suffering were not part of God's original plan, they'll be more likely to trust God and the goodness of his will for their lives. When kids realize that God's goodness is greater than any evil, they'll be able to withstand the worst temptation and the most painful circumstance.

Satan has a plan for the lives of your teenagers, and he most likely will try to get them there through **teen experimentation.** In the first study, your students will be challenged to see that the seemingly harmless choices they make concerning evil and morality can have dire consequences.

The second study tackles a tough but very important issue: **the occult.** Many kids seem to think the occult is just a game. It's important to help them see that playing with evil is dangerous and they need to be careful about "dabbling" in evil.

The third study challenges kids to guard their hearts and minds from moral evil. Teenagers will examine the detriments and dangers of **horror.** They'll be challenged to focus on good things to keep their hearts and minds pure.

Satan is real and active. He uses **deception** to trap people into pain and self-destruction. The final study will help your kids stand strong against Satan's pleasant, subtle, and dangerous lies.

Sooner or later everyone has to face evil. If your young people haven't wrestled with it already, they will. A biblical perspective on evil will help your kids avoid naiveté and self-pity. And it'll enable them to explain the existence of evil in a world created and sustained by a good, loving God.

*For a more comprehensive look at this Core Christian Belief, read Group's **Get Real: Making Core Christian Beliefs Relevant to Teenagers.***

DEPTHFINDER
HOW THE BIBLE DESCRIBES EVIL

- **Any deviation from God's character or will is evil.** Only God is good, and he wishes only good for his creation. So any action or event that does not conform to God's good character or good intention is evil (2 Chronicles 7:3; Psalms 34:8; 119:65-68; Mark 10:18; Romans 12:2; and 1 Peter 2:1-3).

- **Evil includes everything sinful (moral evil) and everything harmful (natural evil).** God created humans to live in communion with him. Sin breaks God's relationship with us, resulting in moral evil. Likewise, God wants all of creation to live in peace and harmony, but natural evil—disease, suffering, death, and destruction—can sometimes work against God's will (Genesis 3:14-19; Psalm 5:4; Ecclesiastes 5:15-17; 6:1-2; Romans 8:7-8; and Ephesians 4:17-19).

- **Moral evil entered God's creation through human disobedience.** God created humans morally good, but they disobeyed God and became morally evil. As a result, we all live with the reality of sin and evil. We disobey God's commands, hurt and abuse others, and love ourselves more than God or our neighbors (Genesis 1:31; 3:1-19; Psalm 53:2-3; Romans 3:9-18, 23; 5:12-19; and James 1:13-15).

- **Natural evil entered the world because of moral evil.** When God's creation was free from moral evil, it was also free from every natural harm. Because of human sin, creation is filled with dangers such as floods, tornadoes, and earthquakes. And every living thing decays and dies (Genesis 1:1–3:19; 6:5-12; Deuteronomy 28:15-24; Romans 5:12-14; 8:19-21; and 1 Timothy 4:4).

- **We experience the effects of moral evil and natural evil.** Sometimes we experience the consequences of our own sin or the sin of others. Other times life is difficult for reasons known only to God or simply because we live in a sin-cursed world (Job 1:1–2:10; Proverbs 29:6; Isaiah 13:9-11; John 9:1-3; and Hebrews 12:7-11).

- **We sin individually and collectively.** Just as natural evil afflicts individuals and groups, moral evil can rule individuals and groups. People sin against God and each other. The powerful oppress or enslave the weak. Nations war against and exploit their own people and the citizens of other nations (Deuteronomy 1:35; Jeremiah 8:3; 13:10; Amos 5:13; Matthew 12:39, 45; 16:4; Luke 11:29; Ephesians 5:16; and 6:13).
- **Satan, the evil one, reigns over evil.** Sinful humans are under the rule of the evil one, but they're still responsible for their sin. However, God limits the power and influence of the evil one. As the ruler of this age, Satan can use natural evil for his own purposes. However, not all natural evil can be blamed on him (Genesis 3:16-19; Matthew 6:13; John 17:15; Ephesians 6:10-16; 1 John 3:12; and 5:18-19).
- **Presently God limits the amount of moral and natural evil.** God does not allow humans to become as evil as they could be. And sometimes God turns human evil into something good. Finally, God spreads good things throughout the creation (Genesis 50:19-20; Job 38:12-15; 40:6-14; Psalm 145:9; Matthew 5:44-45; and Acts 14:15-17).
- **Eventually God will remove moral evil and restore his creation to a naturally good state.** God will resurrect all people: the evil to be judged and the righteous to live in a state of natural goodness. God will also defeat the evil one and banish him forever. In the end, heaven and earth will be completely good (Isaiah 11:1-9; Hosea 2:18; John 5:28-29; 12:31; Romans 8:22-23; and Revelation 20:7–21:4).

CORE CHRISTIAN BELIEF OVERVIEW

Here are the twenty-four Core Christian Belief categories that form the backbone of Core Belief Bible Study Series:

The Nature of God	Jesus Christ	The Holy Spirit
Humanity	Evil	Suffering
Creation	The Spiritual Realm	The Bible
Salvation	Spiritual Growth	Personal Character
God's Justice	Sin & Forgiveness	The Last Days
Love	The Church	Worship
Authority	Prayer	Family
Service	Relationships	Sharing Faith

Look for Group's Core Belief Bible Study Series books in these other Core Christian Beliefs!

about core belief

Bible Study Series
for junior high/middle school

Think for a moment about your young people. When your students walk out of your youth program after they graduate from junior high or high school, what do you want them to know? What foundation do you want them to have so they can make wise choices?

You probably want them to know the essentials of the Christian faith. You want them to base everything they do on the foundational truths of Christianity. Are you meeting this goal?

If you have any doubt that your kids will walk into adulthood knowing and living by the tenets of the Christian faith, then you've picked up the right book. All the books in Group's Core Belief Bible Study Series encourage young people to discover the essentials of Christianity and to put those essentials into practice. Let us explain...

What Is Group's Core Belief Bible Study Series?

Group's Core Belief Bible Study Series is a biblically in-depth study series for junior high and senior high teenagers. This Bible study series utilizes four defining commitments to create each study. These "plumb lines" provide structure and continuity for every activity, study, project, and discussion. They are:

● **A Commitment to Biblical Depth**—Core Belief Bible Study Series is founded on the belief that kids not only *can* understand the deeper truths of the Bible but also *want* to understand them. Therefore, the activities and studies in this series strive to explain the "why" behind every truth we explore. That way, kids learn principles, not just rules.

● **A Commitment to Relevance**—Most kids aren't interested in abstract theories or doctrines about the universe. They want to know how to live successfully right now, today, in the heat of problems they can't ignore. Because of this, each study connects a real-life need with biblical principles that speak directly to that need. This study series finally bridges the gap between Bible truths and the real-world issues kids face.

● **A Commitment to Variety**—Today's young people have been raised in a sound bite world. They demand variety. For that reason, no two meetings in this study series are shaped exactly the same.

● **A Commitment to Active and Interactive Learning**—Active learning is learning by doing. Interactive learning simply takes active learning a step further by having kids teach each other what they've learned. It's a process that helps kids internalize and remember their discoveries.

For a more detailed description of these concepts, see the section titled "Why Active and Interactive Learning Works With Teenagers" beginning on page 57.

So how can you accomplish all this in a set of four easy-to-lead Bible studies? By weaving together various "power" elements to produce a fun experience that leaves kids challenged and encouraged.

Betrayed!

HELPING KIDS DEAL WITH REJECTION FROM THE PEOPLE THEY LOVE

by Jennifer Correll

THE POINT:

God is love.

■ Betrayal has very little shock value for this generation. It's as commonplace as compact discs and mosh pits. For many kids today, betrayal characterizes their parents' wedding vows. It's part of their curriculum at school; it defines the headlines and evening news. Betrayal is not only accepted—it's expected. ■ At the heart of such acceptance lies the belief that nothing is absolute. No vow, no law, no promise can be trusted. Relationships are betrayed at the earliest convenience. Repeatedly, kids see that something called "love" lasts just as long as it's ... permanence. But deep inside, they hunger to see a

---

The Study
AT A GLANCE

SECTION	MINUTES	WHAT STUDENTS WILL DO	SUPPLIES
Discussion Starter	up to 5	JUMP-START—Identify some of the most common themes in today's movies.	Newsprint, marker
Investigation of Betrayal	12 to 15	REALITY CHECK—Form groups to compare anonymous, real-life stories of betrayal with experiences in their own lives.	"Profiles of Betrayal" handouts (p. 20), highlighter pens, newsprint, marker, tape
	3 to 5	WHO BETRAYED WHOM?—Guess the identities of the people profiled in the handouts.	Paper, tape, pen
Investigation of True Love	15 to 18	SOURCE WORK—Study and discuss God's definition of perfect love.	Bibles, newsprint, marker
	5 to 7	LOVE MESSAGES—Create unique ways to send a "message of love" to the victims of betrayal they've been studying.	Newsprint, markers, tape
Personal Application	10 to 15	SYMBOLIC LOVE—Give a partner a personal symbol of perfect love.	Paper lunch sack, pens, scissors, paper, catalogs

notes:

- **A Relevant Topic**—More than ever before, kids live in the now. What matters to them and what attracts their hearts is what's happening in their world at this moment. For this reason, every Core Belief Bible Study focuses on a particular hot topic that kids care about.

- **A Core Christian Belief**—Group's Core Belief Bible Study Series organizes the wealth of Christian truth and experience into twenty-four Core Christian Belief categories. These twenty-four headings act as umbrellas for a collection of detailed beliefs that define Christianity and set it apart from the world and every other religion. Each book in this series features one Core Christian Belief with lessons suited for junior high or senior high students.

  "But," you ask, "won't my kids be bored talking about all these spiritual beliefs?" No way! As a youth leader, you know the value of using hot topics to connect with young people. Ultimately teenagers talk about issues because they're searching for meaning in their lives. They want to find the one equation that will make sense of all the confusing events happening around them. Each Core Belief Bible Study answers that need by connecting a hot topic with a powerful Christian principle. Kids walk away from the study with something more solid than just the shifting ebb and flow of their own opinions. They walk away with a deeper understanding of their Christian faith.

- **The Point**—This simple statement is designed to be the intersection between the Core Christian Belief and the hot topic. Everything in the study ultimately focuses on The Point so that kids study it and allow it time to sink into their hearts.

- **The Study at a Glance**—A quick look at this chart will tell you what kids will do, how long it will take them to do it, and what supplies you'll need to get it done.

● **The Bible Connection**—This is the power base of each study. Whether it's just one verse or several chapters, The Bible Connection provides the vital link between kids' minds and their hearts. The content of each Core Belief Bible Study reflects the belief that the true power of God—the power to expose, heal, and change kids' lives—is contained in his Word.

THE POINT OF *BETRAYED!*:

God is love.

1 JOHN 4:7-21   The Apostle John explains the nature and definition of perfect love.

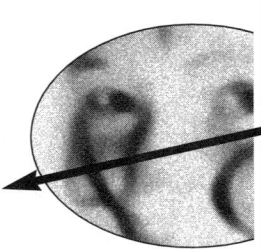

I n this study, kids will compare the imperfect love defined in real-life stories of betrayal to God's definition of perfect love.

By making this comparison, kids can discover that God is love and therefore incapable of betraying them. Then they'll be able to recognize the incredible opportunity God off relationship worthy of their absolute trust.

Explore the verses in The Bible Connection mation in the Depthfinder boxes throughout understanding of how these Scriptures conne

LEADER TIP

THE STUDY

DISCUSSION STARTER ▼

Jump-Start (up to 5 minutes) As kids arrive, ask them to thin common themes in movies, books, TV show have kids each contribute ideas for a mast li two other kids in the room and sharing eir fi sider providing copies of People maga e to what's currently showing on television or at the their suggestions, write their respon s on new **come up with a lot of great ide . Even tho ent, look through this list and ry to discov ments most of these themes ave in comm

After kids make several su estions, mention responses are connected w h the idea of betray

● **Why do you think etrayal is such a co**

LEADER TIP for The Study

Because this topic can be so powerful and relevant to kids' lives, your group members may be tempted to get caught up in issues and lose sight of the deeper biblical principle found in The Point. Help your kids grasp The Point by guiding kids to focus on the biblical investigation and discussing how God's truth connects with reality in their lives.

DEPTHFINDER   **UNDERSTANDING INTEGRITY**

Y our students may not be entirely familiar with the meaning of integrity, especially as it might apply to God's character in the Trinity. Use these definitions (taken from Webster's II New Riverside Dictionary) and other information to help you guide kids toward a better understanding of how God maintains integrity through the three expressions of the Trinity.

Integrity: 1. Firm adherence to a code or standard of values. 2. The state of being unimpaired. 3. The quality or condition of being undivided.

Synonyms for integrity include probity, completeness, wholeness, soundness, and perfection.

Our word "integrity" comes from the Latin word *integritas*, which means soundness. *Integritas* is also the root of the word "integer," which means "whole or complete," as in a "whole" number.

The Hebrew word that's often translated "integrity" (for example, in Psalm 25:21 [NIV]) is *tam*. It means whole, perfect, sincere, and honest.

● **Depthfinder Boxes**—These informative sidelights located throughout each study add insight into a particular passage, word, historical fact, or Christian doctrine. Depthfinder boxes also provide insight into teen culture, adolescent development, current events, and philosophy.

CREATIVE GOD-EXPLORATION ▼

Top Hats (18 to 20 minutes) Form three groups, with each trio member from the previous activity going to a different group. Give each group Bibles, paper, and pens, and assign each group a different hat God wears: Father, Son, or Holy Spirit.

● **Leader Tips**—These handy information boxes coach you through the study, offering helpful suggestions on everything from altering activities for different-sized groups to streamlining discussions to using effective discipline techniques.

holy Profiles

Your assigned Bible passage describes how a particular person or group responded when confronted with God's holiness. Use the information in your passage to help your group discuss the questions below. Then use your flashlights to teach the other two groups what you discover.

■ Based on your passage, what does holiness look like?

■ What does holiness sound like?

■ When people see God's holiness, how does it affect them?

■ How is this response to God's holiness like humility?

■ Based on your passage, how would you describe humility?

■ Why is humility an appropriate human response to God's holiness?

■ Based on what you see in your passage, do you think you are a humble person? Why or why not?

■ What's one way you could develop humility in your life this week?

● **Handouts**—Most Core Belief Bible Studies include photocopiable handouts to use with your group. Handouts might take the form of a fun game, a lively discussion starter, or a challenging study page for kids to take home—anything to make your study more meaningful and effective.

The Last Word on Core Belief Bible Studies

Soon after you begin to use Group's Core Belief Bible Study Series, you'll see signs of real growth in your group members. Your kids will gain a deeper understanding of the Bible and of their own Christian faith. They'll see more clearly how a relationship with Jesus affects their daily lives. And they'll grow closer to God.

But that's not all. You'll also see kids grow closer to one another.

That's because this series is founded on the principle that Christian faith grows best in the context of relationship. Each study uses a variety of interactive pairs and small groups and always includes discussion questions that promote deeper relationships. The friendships kids will build through this study series will enable them to grow *together* toward a deeper relationship with God.

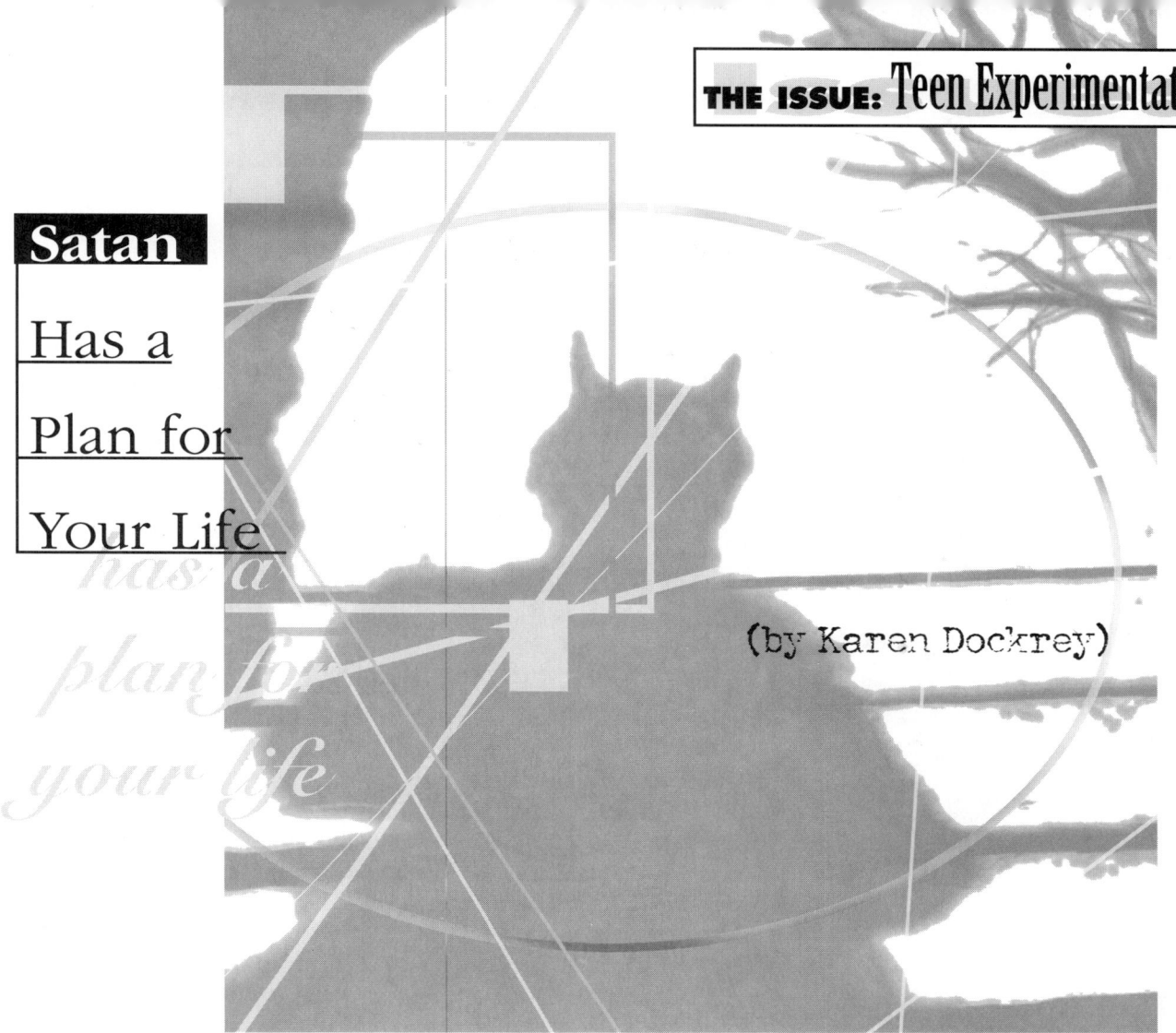

Satan Has a Plan for Your Life

has a plan for your life

(by Karen Dockrey)

■ "Just take one hit—you'll love it." ■ "C'mon, one drink won't hurt." ■ "Meet me after school behind the gym. I got a whole pack of cigarettes from my mom's purse." ■ Temptation. It's everywhere, and your junior highers experience it in large doses. Sometimes temptation starts with the desire to be accepted. Sometimes it's sparked by curiosity about the forbidden or the unknown. ■ Whatever the reasons, young people ex-

THE POINT:

Satan has a plan for your life.

periment with behaviors that put themselves at risk—risk of physical harm and of emotional wounds. ■ But there's an even greater risk—the risk of falling into Satan's nefarious grip. ■ This study helps your young people realize that experimenting with risky behaviors makes them vulnerable to Satan's plan for their lives, which is to live separated from God for eternity. But your students don't have to make themselves susceptible to Satan's influence. By God's power they can resist the devil's schemes.

The Study
AT A GLANCE

SECTION	MINUTES	WHAT STUDENTS WILL DO	SUPPLIES
Discovery Game	10 to 15	RISKY LISTS—Create index-card chains listing dangerous risks young people might take.	Index cards, pencils, masking tape
Creative Bible Exploration	20 to 25	SEE THE SCHEMES—Draw storyboards from end to beginning to show how Satan tried to fulfill his plan for certain people in the Bible.	Bibles, long sheets of newsprint, markers, tape
Practicing Resistance	10 to 15	LEVELING SATAN'S LINES—Practice resisting dangerous dares and help each other develop strong responses to dares.	"Level the Lines" handouts (p. 22), scissors, paper lunch bags
Positive Risk-Taking	up to 5	CHOOSE REAL RISK—Take a risk by encouraging each other.	

notes:

Satan has a plan for your life.

THE BIBLE CONNECTION

GENESIS 3	Adam and Eve give in to Satan's temptation to eat forbidden fruit and reap the consequences of separation from God.
LUKE 4:1-13	Jesus resists Satan's temptations through God's power and Word.
1 CORINTHIANS 10:13; **HEBREWS 4:14-15;** **1 PETER 5:8-9**	Christians can resist Satan's schemes through faith and God's power.

I n this study, kids will explore the schemes Satan uses to tempt them into taking harmful risks.

Through this exploration, kids will discover how to recognize Satan's strategies and how to resist Satan's temptations through God's power.

Explore the verses in The Bible Connection, then study the information in the Depthfinder boxes throughout the study to gain a deeper understanding of how these Scriptures connect with your young people.

LEADER TIP for The Study

Whenever groups discuss a list of questions, write the questions on newsprint, and tape the newsprint to the wall so groups can discuss the questions at their own pace.

THE STUDY

DISCOVERY GAME ▼

Risky Lists (10 to 15 minutes) After everyone has arrived, have students form teams of four, and hand each team a stack of index cards, a pencil, and a six-foot strip of masking tape. Say: **I'd like your team to make a "chain" of dangerous risks that could hurt you or someone else. Make this chain by listing as many risks as you can on index cards, writing**

**RISKY LISTS
INDEX-CARD
CHAIN**

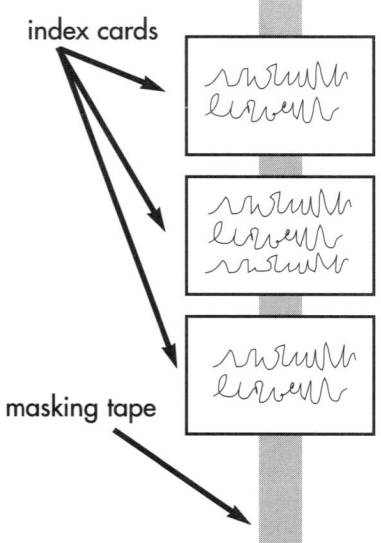

index cards

masking tape

one risk per card. Then stick the cards to the masking tape, creating a chain of index cards. I challenge you to be the team with the longest chain. Ready? Go!

After two minutes, have teams hold up their chains and read the risks they thought of. Then determine which team came up with the most risks.

Have teams discuss these questions:

● **What similarities do you see in the risks listed on your chains? differences?**

● **What makes taking risks attractive?**

● **Which risks are you most prone to take? Explain.**

● **What's the most dangerous risk you've ever been tempted to take? Did you take it? Why or why not?**

Instruct each team to wrap one member in the index-card chain. (Make extra tape available in case teams need it.) Say: **When someone challenges us to do something, we like to take the challenge. But just as some of you are bound by a paper chain of risks, experimenting with risky behaviors such as drinking or having premarital sex can bind us. We might not understand how they bind us until we're already too far gone. And that's exactly the way the devil wants it. <u>Satan has a plan for your life</u>, and without your knowledge, he can encourage you to try things that will hurt you. Today we'll explore how some risks lure us into Satan's plan.**

Have teams pray together that God will open their eyes to Satan's schemes for enticing them away from God and closer to himself. Then have foursomes remove the index-card chains from their team members and tape their chains to a wall in the meeting room.

DEPTH FINDER UNDERSTANDING SATAN'S INFLUENCE

How do you know when Satan's plan is being fulfilled in a student's life? Youth worker and author Rick Chromey, in a GROUP Magazine article "Seduced by Satan," lists seven signs that indicate your students might be walking that dangerous path toward Satan:

1. frequent listening to music with death themes and satanic images;

2. possession of occult-oriented items such as jewelry featuring a goat's head or a pentagram;

3. possession of books about the occult and witchcraft;

4. involvement with occult games such as fantasy games or boards that conjure up spirits;

5. drug and/or alcohol abuse;

6. personality changes—especially declining school performance, violent rages, and withdrawal from family and friends; and

7. self-mutilation.

If one of your students exhibits any of these characteristics, begin praying that the Holy Spirit will help that student see how Satan is working a dangerous plan in his or her life. Confront that student with the truth that God's power is greater than Satan's and that God wants to give life. Also seek counsel and prayer support from committed youth leaders you trust as you deal with this student.

CREATIVE BIBLE EXPLORATION ▼

See the Schemes
(20 to 25 minutes)

Have students remain in their foursomes from the previous activity. Assign half of the groups to read Genesis 3 and the other half to read Luke 4:1-13. As they read, give each group a long sheet of newsprint and some markers.

When groups have finished reading, say: **Create a storyboard expressing the story you read in your Bible passage, but create it from the end of the story to the beginning. Begin by drawing the last frame first, telling how the story ended. Then draw the next-to-the-last frame showing what led to the ending of the story. As you do this, think of how Satan had a plan for the people in your Bible story, how he tried to fulfill that plan, how the people responded, and the consequences of their responses.**

When groups have finished, have them tape their storyboards to the wall. Then have each group meet with a group that studied the other Bible story. Have groups explain their storyboards to each other from the ending to the beginning, including the results of the story, how Satan tempted the people in the story, and how the people were or were not vulnerable to Satan's schemes. As groups teach each other, tape a fresh sheet of newsprint to the wall and draw two vertical lines, dividing the paper into three equal sections.

Then have the whole group gather together. Ask students to call out the schemes Satan used to tempt Adam and Eve and Jesus, and write these schemes on the left section of the newsprint. Then have kids call out ways Adam and Eve allowed Satan to fulfill his plan for their lives. List these ways in the middle column. Finally, have students call out ways Jesus avoided Satan's plan for his life, and list these ways in the right column of the newsprint. If students struggle with any of these lists, mention one or two ideas from the "Reacting to Satan's Schemes" Depthfinder (p. 20) to get them started.

Say: **Satan may have a plan for our lives, but as Jesus showed us, we don't have to follow his plan. We choose the ending to our tempting situations. We don't have to be fooled as Adam and Eve were. We have access to the same power Jesus had—God's power that's available to all Christians.**

Tell kids to think of a temptation they've faced. Have them refer to the index-card chains they created in the "Risky Lists" activity if they need ideas.

Then have each student turn to a partner and answer these questions:
● **What was the ending to your temptation story?**
● **Does focusing on the endings of temptation stories help you avoid falling into temptation? Explain.**
● **What strategy did Satan use to tempt you into taking that risk?**
● **What were (or would have been) the results of taking the risk?**
● **How might Satan have used that situation to fulfill his plan for your life?**
● **How would you handle that situation if you were in it again today?**

Have students return to their foursomes to read 1 Corinthians 10:13;

LEADER TIP for The Study

Because this topic can be so powerful and relevant to kids' lives, your group members may be tempted to get caught up in issues and lose sight of the deeper biblical principle found in The Point. Help your kids grasp The Point by guiding kids to focus on the biblical investigation and discussing how God's truth connects with reality in their lives.

Hebrews 4:14-16; and 1 Peter 5:8-9 and discuss these questions:

● **What truths from these passages can help you withstand Satan's dares?**

● **How might Satan tempt you in the coming week?**

● **What's one truth from these passages that you'll remember when you face temptation?**

Say: <u>Satan has a plan for your life</u>, **and he's crafty in trying to fulfill it. He'll find every way he can to trip you up. But God is stronger than Satan, and as you have faith in God and call on his power to resist temptation, you can avoid Satan's plan.**

Have foursomes pray to thank God for this power and to ask for his help when they're tempted.

DEPTH FINDER — REACTING TO SATAN'S SCHEMES

We can learn how to avoid Satan's dares by exploring Scriptures revealing his schemes, people's responses to his schemes, and the consequences of those responses. Here are two prime examples:

SCRIPTURE	SATAN'S SCHEMES	RESPONSES TO THOSE SCHEMES	CONSEQUENCES
Adam and Eve (Genesis 3)	● Satan made God's rules seem more restrictive than they were. ● Satan lied about the consequences of giving in to temptation. ● Satan encouraged doubt about the purity of God's motives in creating his rules.	● Eve looked at the situation from Satan's point of view. ● Eve continued to talk to Satan even though he had told her things she knew weren't true.	● Adam and Eve both gave in to the temptation to eat the forbidden fruit, and God cast them (and the rest of humanity) from the Garden of Eden.
Jesus (Luke 4:1-13)	● Satan played on Jesus' immediate need (hunger) by tempting him to create bread from a rock. ● Satan played on a universal desire for power. ● Satan misquoted Scripture to try to convince Jesus to jump off the temple.	● Jesus correctly quoted Bible passages to combat the arguments Satan presented. ● Jesus remained firm, saying no to each of Satan's temptations.	● Jesus successfully resisted Satan's temptations, keeping himself absolutely pure so he could be the holy sacrifice for all our sins.

While Adam and Eve failed to resist Satan's temptations, Jesus provided us with a prime example of how to handle Satan when he tempts us. Jesus also provided us with victory over Satan for all time by dying on the cross and rising again.

PRACTICING RESISTANCE ▼

Leveling Satan's Lines
(10 to 15 minutes)
Before the study, make one photocopy of the "Level the Lines" handout (p. 22) for every four students. Cut the "lines" or statements apart, fold them in half, and put each set of statements into a separate paper lunch bag.

LEADER TIP
for Leveling Satan's Lines
For added fun, give each group a bell or horn to signal when a person needs to come up with a stronger answer.

Say: **Whenever you make a plan to resist Satan, he'll try to defeat you. Satan has a plan for your life, and if he can discourage you from resisting him, he'll have an easier time fulfilling his plan. Let's practice ways to respond when Satan tempts us.**

Have kids form a circle with their foursomes. Give each group one of the paper lunch bags full of lines. Say: **When I say "go," the person who's holding the bag should pass the bag to the person on his or her right. Keep passing the bag around the circle until I shout, "I dare ya!" When I shout that phrase, the person who's holding the bag must pull a slip of paper from the bag, read aloud the dare on the paper, then respond to it with a truth about why he or she shouldn't take that dare.**

Groups, as your person responds, help him or her. If he or she makes a statement that would effectively fend off the dare, clap and cheer. If you think your person's response could be stronger, make a game show buzzer noise; then work together with your person to come up with a stronger truth.

Have kids play the game for up to six rounds. Then have groups discuss these questions:

● **What was it like to come up with a truth on your own?**

● **How did it feel to have fellow group members help you come up with stronger truths?**

● **How was helping each other come up with truths like helping each other avoid dangerous dares in real life?**

● **What's one thing you can do this week to help a friend resist a dare?**

Say: **Satan has a plan for your life, and when you stand alone against him, it's harder to resist his dares. But friends can help each other resist Satan through encouragement and prayer.**

POSITIVE RISK-TAKING ▼

Choose Real Risk
(up to 5 minutes)
Say: **Not all risks are bad. In fact, some risks can make us feel better about ourselves or can help us build real friendships. I dare you to tell the other members of your group why you're glad you're in the same group—for example, "Chris, I'm glad we're in the same group because you have good ideas for resisting dangerous dares."**

Have groups pray together that God will help them resist Satan's plan for their lives.

Level the Lines

"C'mon, take a **drink or two.**
Don't you want to have *fun?"*

"Go ahead and *take your dad's car.*
You're **just** *going around the block."*

"Because we *love* each other, it's OK for us to show it.
Just this once won't hurt."

"Go ahead and *lie to your parents.*
Everybody does it."

"Go ahead and smoke мarijuaNa.
Nothing will happen."

"You've got a good reason to cheat.
Don't be so worried."

Enamored With Evil

by Rick Chromey

The Truth About the Occult

■ Power. Who doesn't want it in some form or another? ■ Junior highers are no different. Stuck between childhood and adulthood, these young people test their boundaries to see what they can achieve. Much of this experimentation can be relatively harmless and reflective of normal adolescent rebellion, such as staying up late or skipping church. ■ But some experimentation is deadly. ■ Satan entices kids into his domain, seducing them with promises of power. He invites them to participate in seemingly innocent activities such as playing with Magic cards or living by horoscopes. Young people experience an intoxicating sense of power and delve deeper into these activities. Soon, without even realizing it, they hand their power over to Satan, and they're more helpless than they've ever been. ■ This study exposes Satan's use of the occult to defeat, deceive, and destroy people. And the study reveals the greater source of power that's available to all of us: God.

THE POINT:

Satan isn't equal to God in power or authority.

The Study
AT A GLANCE

SECTION	MINUTES	WHAT STUDENTS WILL DO	SUPPLIES
Creative Opener	10 to 15	SATAN A-SALT—Make and taste punch seasoned with salt.	Pitchers, water, paper cups, punch mix, bowls, salt, stirring utensils, "How to Make Punch" handouts (p. 31)
Bible Discovery	30 to 40	MORE TRICK THAN TREAT—Experience object lessons that illustrate how Satan tries to defeat, deceive, and destroy people.	Bibles, pastries, plastic wrap, black construction paper or garbage bags, towels, votive candle, matches, balloons, markers, tape, newsprint
Reflective Prayer	5 to 10	THE WAY, TRUTH, AND LIFE—Creatively thank Jesus for defeating Satan.	

notes:

Satan isn't equal to God in power or authority.

THE BIBLE CONNECTION

EZEKIEL 28:11-19	Ezekiel prophesies about Satan's nature.
JOHN 14:6	Jesus proclaims his role as the way, the truth, and the life.
2 CORINTHIANS 11:14	Paul explains that Satan "masquerades as an angel of light."
HEBREWS 2:14-15	The writer of Hebrews explains that Jesus defeated the devil.
1 PETER 5:8-10	Peter explains that if we resist the devil, God will restore us.

I n this study, kids will explore how Satan uses seemingly harmless occult activities to draw people into his web of deception, defeat, and destruction. Students will compare Satan's deadly power to the life-giving power we can have because of Jesus' death on the cross and resurrection from the grave.

By making this comparison, kids can discover that God's power and authority is greater than Satan's—much greater than the false power kids experience through the occult.

Explore the verses in The Bible Connection, then examine the information in the Depthfinder boxes throughout the study to gain a deeper understanding of how these Scriptures connect with your young people.

BEFORE THE STUDY

For the "Satan A-Salt" Creative Opener, gather one set of the following supplies for every four students: a copy of the "How to Make Punch" handout (p. 31), four empty paper cups, one pitcher of water, one packet of punch mix, a stirring utensil, and a bowl with one cup of salt in it. Place the sets of ingredients in different locations around your room. If your meeting room is carpeted, you might want to lay a tarp or sheet of plastic on the floor in case kids spill their drinks.

For "More Trick Than Treat," buy one pastry (or doughnut) for every four students. The more tempting the pastries are, the better. Individually wrap each pastry in plastic wrap. Also darken the room by covering windows with black construction paper or garbage bags and placing towels along cracks under the doors.

LEADER TIP
for The Study

Satan doesn't want your young people to learn how he uses deception to gain power over them. Prior to the meeting pray for protection, wisdom, and clarity of purpose. Pray for your students by name, asking the Holy Spirit to guard their hearts before, during, and after the study. Continue to pray as you lead the study.

THE STUDY

LEADER TIP
for Satan A-Salt

A few students may suggest you tricked them into drinking salt-laden punch. But you didn't—you spoke of the salt as "white stuff" and your students assumed it was sugar. Your students' failure to "test everything" (1 Thessalonians 5:21) created the problem. Use the discussion questions to help students learn from this teachable moment.

LEADER TIP
for Satan A-Salt

One of your students may taste the salt before it's added to the drink mixture. If this happens, don't worry. In fact, affirm this young person. Your student took a risk, stepped out on his or her own, and discerned that the white stuff wasn't sugar. Take a moment and encourage your students to question circumstances and make wise choices.

CREATIVE OPENER ▼

Satan A-Salt (10 to 15 minutes)
After everyone has arrived, say: **We have a very special study today, and to start it out, let's prepare some punch for ourselves.** Have kids form foursomes. Have each foursome go to one of the sets of ingredients you set out before the study and follow the instructions on the "How to Make Punch" handout (p. 31) to make the punch. Remind kids to wait to drink their punch so everyone can drink together. When groups are ready, count down from three to one, and have everyone take a gulp at once.

After students have tasted the punch (and the ensuing chaos has died down), have groups discuss these questions:
- **Did you drink the punch? Why or why not?**
- **What's your reaction to your choice?**
- **Have you ever experienced the same reaction in life? If so, what happened?**
- **How is the salt-seasoned punch like occult activities such as fortunetelling and horoscopes? different?**
- **Does Satan ever trick you into believing or doing something wrong? Explain.**
- **How do Satan's deceptions help him gain power over people?**

After five minutes of discussion, say: **Today we're going to examine ways Satan tries to defeat, deceive, and destroy us. Specifically, we'll look at the occult—the hidden, secret, mysterious spirit world. Through this study, we'll discover that no matter how hard Satan tries, he can't gain power over us when we trust in God because <u>Satan isn't equal to God in power or authority</u>.**

BIBLE DISCOVERY ▼

More Trick Than Treat (30 to 40 minutes)
Have kids brainstorm different occult activities while you write their ideas on newsprint taped to a wall.

Say: **Satan will do anything to hinder us from learning the truth about him or his strategies for defeating us. Let's protect ourselves in prayer.** Pray aloud for God's protection from Satan during this study and for everyone to have an open mind to understand what the Bible says about the occult.

Have students remain in their foursomes from the previous activity. Have groups open their Bibles to Ezekiel 28:11-19. Say: **This Bible passage compares an earthly king of Tyre to the devil. As a group,** read the passage and look for everything it says about who Satan is, what he used to be, and what his future is.

As groups do this, tape another sheet of newsprint to a wall. After two minutes, have groups report what they discovered as you write their discoveries on the newsprint. Then say: **The Bible also describes Satan as an accuser, an adversary, the "Evil One," and a tempter. He wants to defeat, deceive, and destroy us. Let's examine each of these objectives.**

Give each group a plastic-wrapped pastry. Have groups look at the list of occult activities and say whether they've been tempted to do any of them. Tell groups that whenever someone speaks, he or she must hold the pastry.

After two minutes, have groups discuss these questions:
● **Were you tempted to eat the pastry when it was passed to you? Why or why not?**
● **If the leader told you the pastry was full of poison, would you still be tempted to eat it? Why or why not?**
● **How is the temptation to eat the pastry like the temptation to engage in occult practices? How is it different?**
● **How might Satan defeat you through temptation?**
Have groups read Matthew 4:1-4, then discuss these questions:
● **How did Jesus counter the devil's temptation?**
● **How would Jesus' strategy work for those involved in occult activities?**
Say: **Satan tempts us to do harmful things by making them seem innocent. This is how he attempts to defeat us. Let's ask God to show us whether we're facing this kind of temptation and, if so, to help us overcome it.**

Pray a brief prayer for wisdom and spiritual guidance to overcome Satan's temptations. Allow students fifteen seconds of silence to pray on their own.

Then ask the entire group to create one large circle. Light a votive candle, turn off the lights, and place the candle in the middle of the circle. Have kids read aloud 2 Corinthians 11:14 together. After kids struggle to decipher the passage for fifteen seconds, turn the lights on again, and have kids complete the activity.

Then have kids return to their foursomes to discuss these questions:
● **Which light is best to read by? Why?**
● **Which light is more like Satan? more like God? Why?**
● **Why would Satan try to look like an "angel of light"?**
● **How does Satan act like an angel of light when enticing people to do the occult activities on our list?**
● **Has Satan ever deceived you about occult activities? If so, how?**
● **What was the result of Satan's deception?**
When groups finish their discussions, pray aloud that God would open kids' eyes to Satan's attempts to deceive them.

Have students remain in their foursomes. Hand each student a balloon. Have students inflate their balloons and write on them their most valuable possessions—for example, "my dog" or "my skateboard." When all group members have finished, have students hand their balloons to the group members across from them and briefly share why

LEADER TIP for The Study

Because this topic can be so powerful and relevant to kids' lives, your group members may be tempted to get caught up in issues and lose sight of the deeper biblical principle found in The Point. Help your kids grasp The Point by guiding kids to focus on the biblical investigation and discussing how God's truth connects with reality in their lives.

LEADER TIP for The Study

Whenever groups discuss a list of questions, write the list on newsprint, and tape it to the wall so groups can discuss the questions at their own pace.

LEADER TIP

for The Study

Some of your students may already be involved in occult activities. Because of this involvement, these students may express objection to parts or all of this study. Some students may disagree that some activities and items are of the occult, such as Halloween or Magic cards. Others may disrupt the meeting or actually leave.

If your students express objections, listen to them, then challenge your young people to listen to you with open minds.

If a student wants to leave, let him or her go freely. Then contact the person after the study to see if he or she wants to talk with you about his or her concerns.

Also keep in mind that some young people might actually attend your lesson to *gain* information about becoming further involved in the occult. Be careful how much specific information you share. You don't want to give your kids the keys to prison.

their possessions are valuable.

When everyone has shared, instruct students to pop the balloons they now hold. Then have groups discuss these questions:

● **How did you feel when your balloon representing your most valuable possession was destroyed by a fellow group member?**

● **Read 1 Peter 5:8-10. How is someone popping your balloon like what Satan wants to do to you? How is it different?**

● **How might Satan use the occult to devour you?**

● **According to the passage, what can you do to avoid destruction by the devil?**

● **How can you do that in the coming week?**

● **How will God help you resist the devil?**

Invite a volunteer to offer a brief prayer of thanksgiving for God's protection against the devil's destruction.

Say: **Satan wants to defeat, deceive, and destroy us. Because of the devil's supernatural power, we might despair of our ability to resist him.** At this point, blow up another balloon. Then say: **But Satan isn't equal to God in power or authority. As we depend on God's protection, we'll win the battles against Satan.** Pop the balloon.

Ask for a volunteer to read aloud Hebrews 2:14-15, then ask:

● **When did Jesus destroy the devil?**

● **What was the result of this act?**

● **How does the devil's destruction impact your desire to give him power in your life through occult activities?**

● **How do you feel knowing that Satan isn't equal to God in power or authority?**

Offer a prayer thanking God for Christ, who destroyed Satan and his power of death and fear.

DEPTHFINDER

SIGNS OF OCCULT INVOLVEMENT

Many young people involve themselves in occultism. Often their involvement is naive and temporary. For some, however, the desire for power and knowledge takes dangerous turns. The steps to occultism are clear. It begins with curiosity and fascination, which sometimes evolves into obsessive behavior with occult ideas, toys, and rituals. Demonic forces, now open to contact, can produce oppression (to secure allegiance) and possibly possession.

According to Neil T. Anderson and Steve Russo, authors of *The Seduction of Our Children*, the following signs reveal curiosity with the occult: withdrawal from usual activities; obsession with death and suicide; extremely low self-image; disinterest in school and/or church; obsession with black; extreme change in friends; obsession with occult symbols, music, literature, or items; drug or alcohol abuse; and extreme fear or anxiety.

Those who are seriously involved also personally possess occult items such as knives or religious artifacts for satanic ceremonies; might have candle wax drippings on their belongings; read books and write journals focusing on death, the occult, Satan-worship, and witchcraft; build altars to Satan in their bedrooms; and may be scarred, burned, cut, or tattooed in satanic ceremonies.

The Way, Truth, and Life

(5 to 10 minutes)
Invite students to lie face up on the floor with their eyes closed. Then say: **We've discovered today how Satan tries to defeat, deceive, and destroy us and uses the occult to achieve these goals. But when we follow Jesus, he frees us from Satan's deceptions. Satan isn't equal to God in power or authority.**

Think of a time when you were tempted to do something wrong but didn't. In John 14:6 Jesus calls himself the way, and you can rely on him as the way to resist temptation. Right now, thank Jesus for helping you overcome temptation in the past, present, and future. As you do, stand up but keep your eyes closed.

When everyone is standing, say: **Perhaps you've participated in occult activities, not realizing they were wrong. Perhaps Satan has deceived you in another way. With your eyes still closed, remember that situation. Jesus states in John 14:6 that he alone is the truth. Thank Jesus for being the truth in your life. Ask his forgiveness for participating in activities or believing lies that go against God's teachings. Ask him to help you see the truth behind Satan's tricks. When you're finished, open your eyes.**

Allow students a moment to think, pray, and open their eyes. When everyone is ready, say: **Many people live empty, difficult lives. Some have been persuaded by Satan that he and his activities are the answer. But Satan's ways lead to death, not life. Jesus says in**

DEPTH FINDER   UNDERSTANDING THE OCCULT

According to Deuteronomy 18:9-13, occultism includes three categories: divination (seeking knowledge of the future), sorcery (seeking power to control others and nature), and spiritism (seeking contact with the dead). Also according to this passage, "The Lord hates anyone who does these things" (verse 12).

Junior highers, often unknowingly, expose themselves to occultism through games, books, movies, music, and even holidays. The following is a brief sampling commonly known to Christians as occult activities. Some are clearly wrong. Others invite kids into deeper occult involvement. And some seem innocent but have occult history or use occult devices.

Divination: tarot cards, Ouija boards, astrology and horoscopes, crystal balls, Halloween.

Sorcery: witchcraft, Magic cards, Satanism, Halloween, fantasy games, New Age mind power, voodoo.

Spiritism: Ouija boards, New Age channeling, automatic writing, movies (such as Ghost), spirit guides, Halloween.

If any of your students are involved in these things, invite them to read Deuteronomy 18:9-13 and 1 Thessalonians 5:21-22 and to ask God to show them his views about their activities. As they seek God's will, encourage them to replace these activities with ones that will draw them nearer to God and his power.

John 14:6 that he is the life. Right now, thank Jesus for giving you life. Or if you know you don't have this life but want it, ask God to help you discover it soon, and feel free to talk about it with me after the meeting.

Allow a moment for introspection, then invite everyone to celebrate! To close, have students form pairs and do the following:

● Share with their partners one thing they learned about Satan.

● Share one way they'll not allow the devil to defeat, deceive, or destroy them in the coming week.

● Share one reason their partners are worth protection from Satan.

● Pray for their partners, asking God to protect and prepare them for battle against Satan in the coming week.

Encourage partners to hold each other accountable and to pray for each other throughout the week.

{ "And no wonder, for *Satan* **himself** masquerades as an *angel of light.*" }

— 2 Corinthians 11:14

Put one packet of the colored stuff in the pitcher of the clear stuff. Then add one bowl of the white stuff. Stir the mixture well. Pick up a paper cup, and pour yourself a drink. Wait until the leader tells you to drink—we're going to have a countdown and drink together.

SCARED TO DEATH
By Trudy Hewitt

■ "I love being scared," is the reason teens often cite for watching horror movies. When pressed further for a reason, some teens say they like the adrenaline rush, while others often have a difficult time explaining their fascination. ■ Horror is everywhere, not only in the movies, but in video games, music, the Internet, books, and comic books. But many junior high students may not realize participating in these activities can be harmful. They may display some resistance to the idea that it's something they shouldn't get involved with. But they may also have experienced a "prick" in their consciences while participating. ■ This study will help kids learn where horror is found, what potential damage or dangers are inherent in it, and why horror is not a good thing. Kids will be given the opportunity to decide where they need to draw the line—even when it's a hard decision.

THE POINT:

Focus on good things.

The Study
AT A GLANCE

the study at a glance

SECTION	MINUTES	WHAT STUDENTS WILL DO	SUPPLIES
Focus Activity	10 to 15	HORROR'S LURE—Participate in a skit demonstrating how Satan uses entertainment to involve us in evil.	"Stop Them!" handouts (pp. 40-41), paper, pens, props (optional)
Bible Connection	10 to 15	UNHEALTHY INTERESTS—Examine and describe opinions on movies and TV, then examine various Scriptures to determine how horror can affect us.	Bibles, "Thoughts About Good and Evil" handouts (p. 42), scissors, paper, pens, markers, newsprint, tape
Bible Reflection	5 to 10	HORROR MEMORIES—Look at how things stay in our brains.	Bibles, tape, black construction paper, white paper, copies of the handout described in the "Before the Study" box
Case Study	5 to 10	TRUE-LIFE HORROR STORIES—Look at true-life stories of how horror led to a dangerous obsession.	

notes:

THE POINT OF "SCARED TO DEATH":

Focus on good things.

THE BIBLE CONNECTION

EPHESIANS 6:12	Paul explains that we are in a spiritual struggle.
PHILIPPIANS 4:8	Paul reminds us to dwell on pure and holy things.
COLOSSIANS 3:5-6	Paul tells us to avoid being controlled by immoral or indecent things.
1 PETER 1:13-16	Peter reminds us to be self-controlled, obedient, and holy.

I n this study, kids will participate in a skit that demonstrates Satan's involvement in horror, discuss various opinions about the effects of television and movies, conduct an experiment that demonstrates how our brains work, and look at how horror has ruined people's lives.

Through this experience kids can discover that they should carefully consider the things they choose to watch and see. They'll also be encouraged to focus on good things.

Explore the verses in The Bible Connection, then examine the information in the Depthfinder boxes throughout the study to gain a deeper understanding of how these Scriptures connect with your young people.

Horror Memories Handout

BEFORE THE STUDY

For the "Unhealthy Interests" activity, set up three stations in your room. Put a stack of one section from the "Thoughts About Good and Evil" handout (p. 42) at each station along with pens, markers, and paper.

For the "Horror Memories" activity, create a handout similar to the diagram in the margin by taping a circle of black construction paper to a white sheet of paper. Make one copy of the handout for each student.

THE STUDY

FOCUS ACTIVITY ▼

LEADER TIP

for Horror's Lure

If you have four kids playing the good kids, have only one "take" the movie ticket, one take the games, and one take the music. Also change the wording from "some were" to "one was."

LEADER TIP

for Horror's Lure

Consider including props for teenagers to use during this skit such as movie tickets, pencils, paper, cards, and CDs.

Horror's Lure (10 to 15 minutes)

Say: **We're going to do a skit about good and evil, and I need everybody to help. I need one person to act as Satan. The rest of you will be "good kids" or act as Satan's demons.**

Have about two-thirds of your students play the good kids and the remaining third act as the demons. Have one student play the part of Satan. Give each student a copy of the "Stop Them!" handout (pp. 40-41).

Say: **Good kids can stand up front and pantomime doing good things, like praying, singing, and reading the Bible. Kids who are playing demons should stand at the back of the room. The person playing Satan will enter when I start to read. I'll read the narrator part, and you'll act out whatever I describe or what's written on your characters' lines of the skit. You'll also need to read your lines.**

After everyone is in place, begin the skit. After the skit ask those who played the demons or Satan:

● **How did it feel playing an evil character?**

● **Do you think Satan and demons really work like this? Explain.**

Ask those who played the good kids:

● **What was it like to be tempted by those playing demons?**

● **How were the choices you made in this skit like or unlike choices you make in real life?**

Ask everyone:

● **Do you think the skit gave an accurate representation of today's entertainment? Why or why not?**

● **How can Satan use entertainment to plant evil in our minds?**

Form groups of three or four and give each group a sheet of paper and a pen. Ask each group to make a list of where horror is found in our society. Give groups one minute for this task. Have each group share some of the examples. Ask:

● **Why do you like or dislike some of the things we've mentioned?**

● **Some people say they've actually felt drawn to horror. What draw do you think horror has for us?**

● **Why would Satan want us to be involved in horror?**

● **Why would God want us to be involved in horror?**

● **Is there a difference in types of horror—are some OK and some not OK? How can we know?**

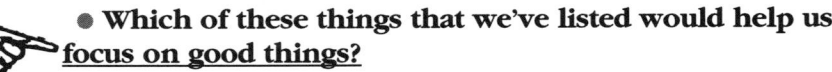 ● **Which of these things that we've listed would help us focus on good things?**

Unhealthy Interests (10 to 15 minutes)

Have students form three groups, and direct each group to one of the three stations you prepared before the study. Say: **At each station are several quotes about the impact movies and TV have on us. Each group will create a picture, in words or graphics, of what the quotes said. You'll bring the picture back to share with the whole group. You have five minutes.**

While kids are in these groups, write the following Scripture references on a sheet of newsprint and tape it to a wall: Ephesians 6:12; Philippians 4:8; Colossians 3:5-6; and 1 Peter 1:13-16.

Have each group present the picture it created and share some of the quotes that inspired the picture. Say: **Now let's see what the Bible has to say about what we watch and see. In your groups, read each of the Scriptures I've listed on the newsprint and come up with a summary of what each Scripture says about what we watch and see.**

After about five minutes, ask:

● **How does watching horror make you feel?**

● **Can watching horror lead you into violence or other problems? Explain.**

● **What kinds of things help us to be holy?**

● **How can what we watch or see help us to be holy?**

LEADER TIP for Unhealthy Interests

If you have more than twenty students, make two sets of the "Thoughts About Good and Evil" sections and set up six stations instead of three.

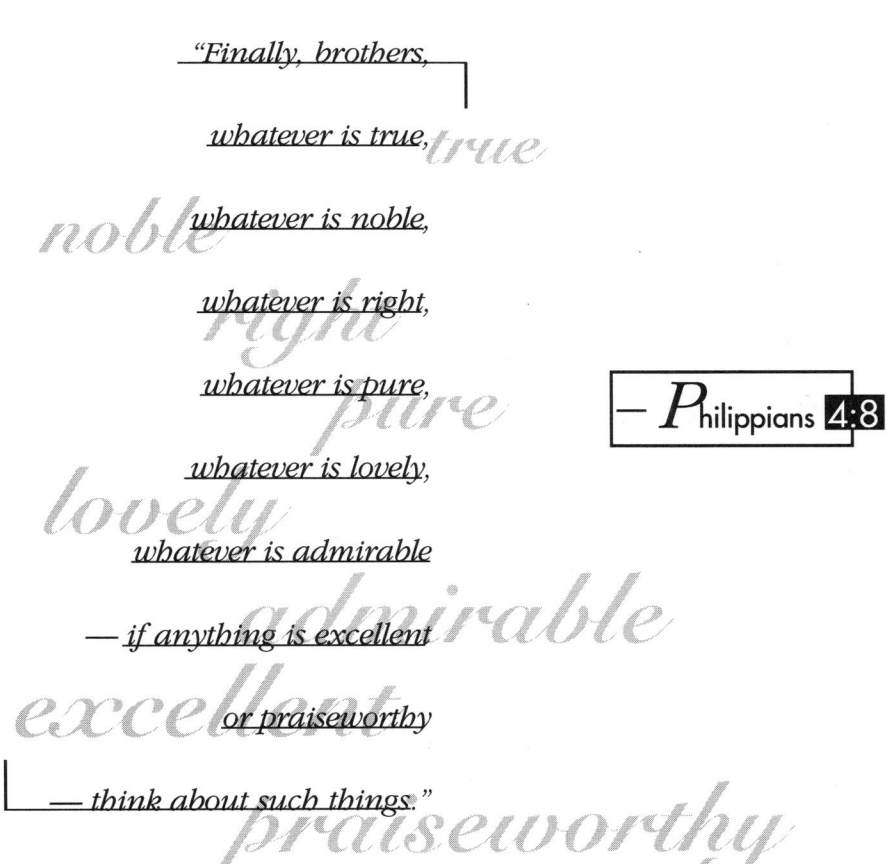

"*Finally, brothers,*
whatever is true,
whatever is noble,
whatever is right,
whatever is pure,
whatever is lovely,
whatever is admirable
— if anything is excellent
or praiseworthy
— think about such things."

*— P*hilippians **4:8**

LEADER TIP

for The Study

Some kids may share opinions counter to God's Word. Don't be defensive. Your job is to share information and God's truth. Teenagers will have to make their own decisions regarding that information.

LEADER TIP

for The Study

Because this topic can be so powerful and relevant to kids' lives, your group members may be tempted to get caught up in issues and lose sight of the deeper biblical principle found in The Point. Help your kids grasp The Point by guiding kids to focus on the biblical investigation and discussing how God's truth connects with reality in their lives.

DEPTH FINDER — UNDERSTANDING YOUR KIDS

We find horror in many places in our society. Kids often don't see a problem playing horror video games or watching horror movies or going to haunted houses. This may be a tough subject and some of them may really struggle with it.

Students are very prone to dabble in sin. They aren't always immersed in it—but some of them get pulled into it anyway. Examine the parable of the sower in Mark 4 to help kids understand that "playing" with things like horror can create the thorns that choke out godly growth.

BIBLE REFLECTION ▼

Horror Memories (5 to 10 minutes)
Give each student a copy of the handout with the black circle you prepared before the study. Have kids stare at the black circle for one minute. Then have kids look at a white wall. Ask:

● **How many of you can see the outline of the circle on the wall?**

● **What does the fact that some of you can still see it say about our memories? our brains?**

● **Picture a sunset,** (pause) **a pen,** (pause) **a scene from a horror film** (pause). **Were you able to picture those items?**

● **What feelings did you have with each picture?**

● **What does that say about the things we should watch or look at?**

Say: **God made our brains in an incredible way. We can store memories and pictures for a long time. However, sometimes when things go into our brains, they don't come out as easily as we'd like. For example, if I asked you to describe some of the scenes from a horror film, could you?** Ask:

● **Do you think it's bad that you can recall those scenes? Explain.**

Ask for a volunteer to read Philippians 4:8 aloud, while kids follow along in their Bibles. Ask:

● **Why do you think we're supposed to think of these types of things?**

● **Does this verse have any bearing on the way you think about horror? Explain.**

● **How would <u>focusing on good things</u> like Paul is saying here affect the things we can picture in our minds?**

True-Life Horror Stories (5 to 10 minutes)

Say: **Of course, it doesn't always happen, but sometimes watching horror movies can lead to a dangerous obsession. Listen to these true stories:**

Mark Branch was nineteen, and he had an impressive collection of horror movies. In fact, police found over ninety of them in his room. They also decided that Mark had stepped over the line into some kind of obsession. They decided that because in his room they found a machete and goalie mask like the ones Jason used in *Friday the 13th*. The police were in Mark's room to search it after Mark killed a female college student and himself. (From David L. Bender, et al., *Violence in the Media.)*

Angel Regino of Los Angeles was picked up after a series of robberies and a murder in which he wore a blue bandanna and fedora identical to those worn by Freddy, the sadistic anti-hero of *Nightmare on Elm Street*. In case anybody missed the significance of his disguise, Regino told his victims that they would never forget him because he was another Freddy Krueger. (From David L. Bender, et al., *Violence in the Media.)* Ask:

● **How can horror lead to an obsession like Mark's or Angel's?**

● **Are there times when horror is OK, or is it always bad? Explain.**

● **How can watching or playing with horror lead to unhealthy obsessions?**

● **Why does God tell us to <u>focus on good things</u>?**

● **What does this mean in your life?**

● **If Mark Branch or Angel Regino had <u>focused on good things</u>, how might it have changed their lives and the lives of their victims?**

Say: **We're going to end our meeting with two questions. Don't answer the questions aloud. Take one minute to silently think them over.** Ask:

● **What attitude toward horror are you going to take from now on?**

● **What action will you take concerning horror?**

LEADER TIP

for The Study

Whenever groups discuss a list of questions, write the questions on newsprint and tape the newsprint to the wall so groups can discuss the questions at their own pace.

DEPTH FINDER — UNDERSTANDING HORROR'S INFLUENCE

C.S. Lewis created the Chronicles of Narnia. He also wrote *The Screwtape Letters*. Following the writing of *Screwtape*, Lewis went into a deep depression for six months. The effort of identifying with a demon in order to pen the letters so filled his mind with evil that a great spiritual battle took place within him.

Narrator: Satan was mad!

Satan: *(Acts out being mad and screams.)* I am so mad!

Narrator: Satan called his demons, and they all came running.

Demons: *(All come running toward Satan from the back of the room.)*

Satan: *(Pointing toward kids)* I want you to go over and look at what those kids are doing.

Demons: *(Surround good kids to see what they're doing.)*

Satan: I really hate it when kids are doing good things!

Narrator: So Satan called his demons back over.

Demons: *(Run back to Satan.)*

Satan: We need a plan.

Demons: *(Hold hands up with a "What should we do?" look.)*

Satan: Stop them! They're doing good. Get them to do evil instead.

Narrator: The demons protested that kids focusing on good things weren't interested in evil.

Satan: We need a scheme.

Narrator: The demons put their heads together.

Demons: *(Pretend to bump heads.)*

Narrator: They tried to come up with a scheme.

Demons: *(Pace and scratch heads, then surround good kids.)*

Narrator: The demons suggested all kinds of evil and disobedient and gross stuff.

Demons: *(Mime making evil suggestions.)*

Narrator: But the good kids were just too busy focusing on good things to hear the evil thoughts, and they ignored the demons.

Good Kids: *(Ignore demons.)*

Narrator: The demons were worried. They paced and wrung their hands.

Demons: *(Wring hands and pace.)*

Narrator: Suddenly the demons figured it out, and they jumped up and down and got excited!

Demons: *(Jump up and down, run over to Satan, and mime telling him something.)*

Satan: So if we make evil seem fun, we'll get the good kids, too? I love your idea! How can we make evil seem fun?

Narrator: The demons put their heads together again.

Demons: *(Pretend to bump heads.)*

Narrator: The demons just weren't sure how to make it look fun, and they began pacing and worrying again.

Demons: *(Pace, worry, and wring hands.)*

Narrator: Suddenly they figured it out!

Demons: *(Jump up and down.)*

Narrator: The demons ran to tell Satan they knew how to get the kids to quit focusing on good things.

Demons: *(Run over to Satan, and mime telling him their idea.)*

Satan: So we could make horror look like entertainment? I really love this idea! Go for it!

Narrator: The demons got busy thinking up movies and games and songs.

Demons: *(Write things, then throw papers in the air before running over to the good kids.)*

Narrator: The demons surrounded the good kids and handed out movie tickets.

Demons: *(Hand out tickets.)*

Narrator: Some of the kids were interested, took the tickets, and left the group to see the movies.

Good Kids: *(One or two take the tickets and leave.)*

Narrator: They brought great evil games.

Demons: *(Pass out games or cards.)*

Narrator: Some more kids left because they wanted to play the games.

Good Kids: *(One or two good kids show interest in the games, take them, and leave.)*

Narrator: They gave out free tapes and CDs.

Demons: *(Give out tapes and CDs.)*

Narrator: A lot of kids liked those, and they left, too.

Good Kids: *(One or two quit what they're doing, look at music, take some, and leave.)*

Narrator: There were only a few kids left doing good things.

Good Kids: *(Look at those who left.)*

Narrator: The demons were satisfied.

Demons: *(Give high fives.)*

Narrator: And Satan was happy.

Satan: *(Acting happy)* I'm happy, happy, happy!

Narrator: The end.

THOUGHTS ABOUT *Good* and *Evil*

Photocopy and cut apart the sections.
Put copies of each section at different stations in your meeting area.

STATION 1

"Ask Sergeant John O'Malley of the New York Police Department about a nine-year-old boy who sprayed a Bronx office building with gunfire. The boy explained to the astonished sergeant how he learned to load his Uzi-like firearm: 'I watch a lot of TV.' " (From David L. Bender, et al., *Violence in the Media.*)

"Watching violence on television is the single best predictor of violent or aggressive behavior later in life." (From David L. Bender, et al., *Violence in the Media.*)

"Televised mayhem is seen as a leading cause of America's epidemic of violent crime." (From David L. Bender, et al., *Violence in the Media.*)

STATION 2

"Two studies published in the New England Journal of Medicine in September 1986 found specific links between television coverage of suicide in movies or news reports and an increased incidence of teenage suicide." (From Gilda Berger, *Violence in the Media.*)

"Children who watch such horror movies appear to become addicted to their own adrenaline. Fear produces a chemical response that acts as a high." (From Phil Phillips, *Saturday Morning Mind Control.*)

"But the main fear that most critics have about violent movies is that they make the audience seek *real* violence." (From Gilda Berger, *Violence and the Media.*)

STATION 3

Senator Paul Simon, a Democrat from Illinois, says, "We now have more people in jail and prison per capita than any country that keeps records, including South Africa...We've spent billions putting people behind bars, and it's had no effect on the crime rate. None. People realize there have to be other answers, and as they've looked around, they have settled on television as one of them." (From David L. Bender, et. al., *Violence in the Media.*)

"Overexposure to manufactured illusions soon destroys their representational power. The illusion of reality dissolves, not in a heightened sense of reality as we might expect, but in a remarkable indifference to reality." (From Christopher Lasch, *The Culture of Narcissism,* quoted in Douglas Davis, *The Five Myths of Television Power.*)

"It is almost impossible to exaggerate the power of the media. We measure power by its effects on those who use it. Who can deny that television, movies, and secular radio programming are having an oppressively harmful influence on the morals of America?" (From Tim LaHaye, *The Hidden Censors.*)

NUDGED off course

by Matt Dirks

■ You went into the car dealership, as strong and stubborn as Captain Ahab. You were just looking. But after learning about the once-in-a-lifetime sale that ended that night, you soon found yourself in a small room signing dozens of papers. The next morning, you saw the same car in the newspaper for thousands less and realized that the deal was less than the incredible bargain you thought you were getting. ■ As much as we detest being deceived, it happens much more than we realize. Every day, we are susceptible to the ploys of the master deceiver—Satan. And many times we fall for his shams. ■ To us, Satan's lies seem innocent and harmless. That's because Satan is also a master counterfeiter. He tricked Eve into thinking sin was acceptable and desirable, and his tactics haven't changed much in the past few millenniums. ■ Your students need to understand just how easily they can be deceived by Satan and his falsehoods—how dangerous Satan's traps really can be and what consequences await those who fall victim to him. They need to see how intent Satan is on leading as many people as he can into their own destruction. ■ But your students also need to know that as powerful as Satan may be, he is a defeated enemy. God has already overthrown Satan's kingdom on earth through the sacrifice of his Son on the cross. And with the Holy Spirit's power, we can resist Satan's deceptions successfully. Salespeople may be another story.

THE POINT:

Satan uses deception to trap people.

The Study
AT A GLANCE
AT A GLANCE

SECTION	MINUTES	WHAT STUDENTS WILL DO	SUPPLIES
Eye Openers	5 to 10	LISTENING TO FISH TALES—Guess the truth of various legends that have been passed around by word-of-mouth.	Fish-shaped crackers
	15 to 20	AVOIDING ICEBERGS AND OTHER DANGERS—Study handouts that briefly describe certain belief systems and try to convince other students of the validity of the beliefs, then discuss the appeal and danger of each belief.	"New Age Movement," "Islam," and "Zen Buddhism" handouts (pp. 52-54), pens
Bible Discovery	15 to 20	CONSULTING THE NAVIGATIONAL CHART—Explore the various ways the Bible says we can be deceived, then think of ways Satan might deceive the average junior higher today and what would make those lies appealing.	Bibles, "How Have You Been Deceived?" handouts (p. 55), pens, newsprint, tape, marker
Reflection and Commitment	10 to 15	NAVIGATING SAFELY THROUGH DANGEROUS WATERS—Think of ways they have been deceived in the past and investigate how God wants them to exercise discernment in the future.	"How Have You Been Deceived?" handouts (p. 55), pens, newsprint, marker

notes:

Satan uses deception to trap people.

THE BIBLE CONNECTION

GALATIANS 6:7-8	There are consequences for our sins.
ROMANS 16:17-18	We can be deceived by people who cause divisions through false teachings.
JAMES 1:16-17	Every good thing comes from God.
JAMES 1:22	We need to hear and do what God's Word says.
1 JOHN 1:8	We are sinful.

I n this study, students will find out some of the ways they have been deceived by common legends, explore the monumental deceptions that have been maintained by major world faiths, discover some of the ways that Scripture tells us we can be deceived, and come up with a "Rule of Life" that will keep them from being deceived in the future.

Through these activities, kids can learn how and why Satan deceives us; what tactics he uses, and what consequences result. They can discover how to use the gift of discernment that God promises to anyone who asks.

Take time to prayerfully explore the passages in The Bible Connection, then examine the information in the Depthfinder boxes throughout the study to gain a deeper understanding of how these Scriptures connect with your young people.

LEADER TIP for The Study

Because this topic can be so powerful and relevant to kids' lives, your group members may be tempted to get caught up in issues and lose sight of the deeper biblical principle found in The Point. Help your kids grasp The Point by guiding kids to focus on the biblical investigation and discussing how God's truth connects with reality in their lives.

THE STUDY

study

EYE OPENERS ▼

Listening to Fish Tales (5 to 10 minutes)

Have the students form two equal-sized teams to play the game Fish Tales. Assign one member of each team to be the captain. Say: **I'm going to read several myths that have been passed around by word-of-mouth for years. You may have heard many of them. Some of them are true, and some are not. After I read one of these legends, your job is to decide as a team whether the statement is true or false. You'll have ten seconds after each legend to decide, then each captain will give the team's response.**

Have each team decide whether they think each of the following urban legends are true or false:

● **If your college roommate commits suicide, you get an automatic 4.0 GPA.** (False. While many colleges offer bereavement considerations under certain circumstances, no college or university in the United States currently has this policy.)

● **In the Chinese language, "Coca Cola" means "I eat wax tadpoles."** (True.)

● **Walt Disney's body was frozen after his death.** (False. Disney's body was cremated after his death.)

● **A fast-food worker was arrested for blowing his nose into a police officer's hamburger.** (True. George J. Kuehme of Phoenix was charged with aggravated assault, adding a harmful substance to food, and disorderly conduct.)

● **Driving barefoot is illegal.** (False. It is not currently illegal to drive barefoot in any of the fifty states. Many states require motorcycle riders to wear shoes.)

● **After eating a can of tuna, a woman removed the label and found a cat-food label underneath.** (True.)

● **We use only 10 percent of our brains.** (False. Humans use only 10 percent of their brains for basic movement and the senses. Therefore, humans have an unusually large brain mass available for higher-level functions.)

● **If you dropped a penny from the top of the Empire State Building, it could kill someone.** (False. Because of the surface area and tendency of a penny to tumble while falling, a penny's terminal velocity is relatively low.)

(Urban legends taken from the San Fernando Valley Folklore Society, www.urbanlegends.com and www.snopes.com.)

After teams have completed voting, pass out fish crackers to everyone, and ask:

● **What surprised you about these legends?**

● **Why do you think so many people believe these legends?**

● **Could being deceived by any of these legends be harmful? Why or why not?**

Say: **These legends are fun little stories that lots of people are deceived by. But many people are also deceived in much more dangerous ways.** Ask:

   ● **How are these legends like or unlike Satan's deceptions?**

   ● **What common deceptions are harmful?**

Say: **Deception is Satan's favorite tool—he is always try- ing to get us to believe something that's not true. Satan uses deception to trap people, and his traps are incredibly dangerous.**

Avoiding Icebergs and Other Dangers

(15 to 20 minutes) Have students form trios. Give each person a pen and a copy of one of the three handouts, "New Age Movement," "Islam," and "Zen Buddhism" (pp. 52-54), so that each trio has all three handouts. Say: **One of Satan's biggest de- ceptions is in the area of faith. He has convinced people all over the world that their beliefs are true. In all of these religions, there are lots of things that are true. But Satan buries his decep- tions in mountains of truth so that we can't distinguish what's true and what's not. It all sounds good.**

Instruct kids to study the handouts they've been given. Tell them to take a few minutes to think through the belief systems they've been

DEPTH FINDER — WHAT THE BIBLE SAYS ABOUT DECEPTION

In Revelation 12:9, Satan is called the one "who leads the whole world astray." In John 8:44, he is called the "father of lies" who "speaks his native language" of falsehood. To Satan, deception is not only a strategy—it is his nature. Satan is like a lion prowling for its victim as he seeks out those who are vulnerable in their faith and those who are spiritually weak. He especially loves to prey on individualists who want to be independent in their faith, and end up alone and unprotected.

We can see Satan's methods in the story of his deception of Eve. She and Adam had received one command from God: "But you must not eat from the tree of the knowledge of good and evil." As Bruce Bickel and Stan Jantz explain in their book *Guide to God: A User-Friendly Approach*, Satan attempted to under- mine this command through a few simple arguments that probably sounded per- fectly logical to Eve:

● "God is placing an unreasonable restriction on you. (He won't let you eat the fruit of that certain tree.)"

● "This restriction is bad because you would be better off without it. (If you eat the fruit, then you will be like God.)"

● "Therefore, God's rule is bad. (He is unfairly restricting your knowledge.)"

● "You would be better off if you didn't pay attention to the restriction. (Eat the fruit. Don't worry, you won't die.)"

Satan is an expert at making us doubt God and ourselves. There is no one bet- ter at making the bad seem good and the good seem bad.

LEADER TIP for Avoiding Icebergs and Other Dangers

When discussing other religions, it is impor- tant to maintain re- spect and love for the people who believe them. Make sure your students do not think that someone is stupid or ignorant for holding to such a belief.

At the same time, make sure you emphasize the distinctive differ- ences between these faiths and Christianity. While many faiths share some basic truths (such as the need for moral purity), only one holds to the need for salvation through Jesus Christ.

LEADER TIP

for The Study

Whenever groups discuss a list of questions, write the questions on newsprint and tape the newsprint to the wall so groups can discuss the questions at their own pace.

given, then take turns trying to convince the other two people in their trios of the validity of their beliefs. Have kids ask the following questions as they study their belief systems:

● **What parts of this belief system make sense?**

● **What are the parts that would sound appealing to the average person?**

Give each trio about ten minutes to complete the exercise, then bring the entire group back together. Ask:

● **What parts of these beliefs sounded appealing to you?**

● **What things do these beliefs have in common with Christianity?**

● **What makes them different from Christianity?**

● **What parts of each belief could be dangerous?**

● **Why do you think Satan would want people to hold to these belief systems?**

Say: **Satan can make anything sound appealing to us. He's the world's greatest salesman, but he's taken the warning labels off of all his products. His sales pitches are just too good to be true. Ultimately, he wants to destroy us. He wants us to experience pain and misery, because then God will experience pain. So Satan uses deception to trap people into destroying themselves.**

BIBLE DISCOVERY ▼

Consulting the Navigational Chart (15 to 20 minutes)

Say: **Even those of us who haven't been deceived by Satan into believing something other than God's truth in the Bible can be deceived in many other areas. The Scriptures give us many examples of how Satan uses deception to trap people.**

Give each student a copy of the "How Have You Been Deceived?" handout (p. 55), a Bible, and a pen, and have kids form trios. Tell kids to complete the top section of the handout by looking up each verse listed and writing down the way the Scripture says we can be deceived. Go through the first verse listed on the handout together, then have trios complete the rest of the section.

Give students enough time to complete the top section of the handout then share what they discovered. Take time to explore what each passage is trying to communicate about deception.

Assign one or two of the passages from the handout to each trio. Say: **Now I want you to come up with at least two examples of ways the average teenager can be deceived in daily life in the area your passage is talking about. For example, if you were assigned Galatians 6:7-8, which talks about the consequences of our sin, you could give examples like how many teenagers think it's OK to lie to their parents as long as they don't get caught or that some teenagers think that experimenting with alcohol isn't really harmful. Write down your ideas under the "Modern-Day**

Deceptions" heading on the handout.

Give each trio time to think up a few examples of how Satan deceives junior highers today. Ask each trio to share its ideas. As trios share, write down their examples on a sheet of newsprint taped to the wall. After each trio has shared, have the whole group decide which of the examples discussed are the three most common ways that Satan deceives teenagers today. Ask:

● **What would make these deceptions sound appealing to the average teenager?**

● **What kind of trap would each of these top three deceptions lead you into?**

● **Are there any other ways in which kids today are often deceived that aren't listed here?**

Say: **Satan has always used deception to trap people. When Adam and Eve ate from the forbidden tree, the only excuse they had to offer God in Genesis 3:13 was "The serpent deceived me, and I ate."** Ask:

● **Why do you think Satan wants to trap people?**

● **What do you think Satan's ultimate goal is?**

Say: **We've seen how <u>Satan uses deception to trap people</u>.**  **Let's look at how God helps us avoid Satan's traps.**

"Do not merely listen to **THE WORD,** and so deceive yourselves. Do what it says."

—James 1:22

Navigating Safely Through Dangerous Waters

(10 to 15 minutes) Share a time in your life when you were deceived into believing or doing something wrong. Then have students look at the examples of areas of deception listed on the newsprint from the "Consulting the Navigational Chart" activity. Have each student think of a time he or she was deceived in one of those areas and record the experience in the "How I've Been Deceived" section of his or her handout. Then have kids share with their trios one of the areas they've encountered deception in. Have students explain the situations they found themselves in and share the consequences that resulted when they fell for Satan's lie.

After the trios have had time to share, say: **The only way we can keep ourselves from being deceived again in the future is by asking God to give us his wisdom and discernment.** Ask:

● **How would you define discernment?**

Get a few ideas of what kids think discernment is, then read aloud the "What the Bible Says About Discernment" Depthfinder (p. 51). Say: **Did you catch that last sentence? Once we ask God for his wisdom, we also need to be willing to follow the guidance he gives us. That's not always easy to do.**

In their trios, have students describe a time when they knew something was wrong but did it anyway. Then have each trio come up with a "Rule of Life" that will help them the next time they encounter a possible deception. Say: **I want you to come up with a simple rule that you'll be able to follow. For example, your rule could be "When I'm not sure if something is right or wrong, I'll**

DEPTH FINDER

WHERE YOUR STUDENTS ARE MOST LIKELY TO BE DECEIVED

Do you think your students are safe from Satan's deceptions because they've grown up in the church? Think again. In a recent survey of churched youth, 54 percent of those surveyed said they believed that "freedom means being able to do anything you want to do, as long as it is legal." Thirty-eight percent said, "lying is sometimes necessary." Thirty-nine percent said, "nothing can be known for certain except the things that you experience in your life." And a whopping 70 percent agreed that "what is right for one person in any given situation might not be right for another person who encounters that same situation." (From Josh McDowell, et al., *Right From Wrong.*)

Obviously, these kids are being exposed to ideas that are far from God's truth. Whether it's by way of a sitcom on TV, a song on the radio, or a teacher at school, America's youth are being deceived *en masse.* One of Satan's favorite deceptions these days seems to be the idea of moral subjectivism. If a junior higher can be persuaded that right and wrong aren't always the same, God's laws become meaningless. A relationship with God becomes no more than a warm fuzzy feeling. And Satan couldn't be happier.

pray for God's guidance and wait to decide until I have peace about it."

After the students have had time to brainstorm, have each trio share its "Rule of Life" with the rest of the group. As each trio shares, write the rule on a sheet of newsprint so that you end up with a complete list of rules to live by. Ask:

● **How can these rules of life help you be more discerning?**

Say: <u>**Satan uses deception to trap people,**</u> **but God gives us discernment to overcome his deception. Let's ask God for the discernment we all need.**

Give kids an opportunity to ask God for discernment in their lives. End the prayer by asking God for his discernment in confusing situations and his discipline to follow the guidance he gives us.

DEPTH FINDER

WHAT THE BIBLE SAYS ABOUT DISCERNMENT

"If any of you lacks wisdom, he should ask God, who gives generously to all without finding fault, and it will be given to him." This statement in James 1:5 is not merely speaking of knowledge. God wants us to ask him for discernment, the ability to tell right from wrong and make wise decisions in confusing situations. When we ask for God's guidance, he is delighted to give it to us.

The difficulty comes in the asking. Many times, we think we can decide for ourselves what's good for our lives. Maybe we'd rather stumble on our own—learning through trial and error. Or maybe we just don't have the faith that God will really answer our prayers.

Whatever the reason, we won't be able to successfully defend ourselves from Satan's strategy of deception until we have learned to humbly and sincerely ask for God's wisdom and direction. And once God gives it to us, we must be committed to following his leading!

New Age Movement

- Every person experiences things and sees things differently, so each person has a different truth. Anything can be true for an individual, but nothing can be true for everyone.

- Each of us needs a radical, personal change in our lives. After we are transformed, each of us can obtain special abilities like healing and psychic powers.

- When enough people experience this change, the world will be changed as well. We will soon live in a kind of heaven on earth, in which the problems of today such as hunger and war are overcome. This will be the "New Age."

(From Richard Kyle, *The Religious Fringe.*)

❖ Allah is the only true God. Jesus was a prophet, just like Moses and Elijah, but Mohammed was a greater prophet.

❖ Because each of us is a sinner, we earnestly worship and follow God through the "Five Pillars of the Faith":

1. Say, "There is no god but Allah and Mohammed is the prophet of Allah."

2. Pray five times a day.

3. Give money to the poor.

4. Fast from all food and drink from sunrise to sunset for one month a year.

5. Make a trip to Mecca, the holy city, at least once during your lifetime.

(From Walter Martin, *The Kingdom of the Cults.*)

ZEN
BUDDHISM

● God is not one person. God is one with everything, and everything is God.

● Each one of us is God, so none of us can sin against God. In fact, there is no such thing as sin.

● We can find our own heaven (called Nirvana) if we keep seeking more wisdom and knowledge. We will be reincarnated (brought back to earth after we die) as many times as it takes for us to reach Nirvana.

● We don't need a Savior, because each of us is responsible for our own destiny.

(From Walter Martin, *The Kingdom of the Cults* and Dr. Peter B. Clarke, ed., *The World's Religions)*

HOW HAVE YOU BEEN DECEIVED?

WHAT THE BIBLE SAYS ABOUT DECEPTION

Look up each of the following verses, then write down how each verse applies to deception:

● Galatians 6:7-8 <u>We can't get away with sin. There are consequences for deception.</u>

● Romans 16:17-18 _____

● James 1:16-17 _____

● James 1:22 _____

● 1 John 1:8 _____

MODERN-DAY DECEPTIONS

Give some examples of ways teenagers can be deceived in the area(s) your trio is looking at.

HOW I'VE BEEN DECEIVED

Write down one time in your life when you were deceived into believing or doing something that was wrong.

why ▼Active and Interactive Learning works with teenagers

Let's Start With the Big Picture

Think back to a major life lesson you've learned.
Got it? Now answer these questions:
- Did you learn your lesson from something you read?
- Did you learn it from something you heard?
- Did you learn it from something you experienced?

If you're like 99 percent of your peers, you answered "yes" only to the third question—you learned your life lesson from something you experienced.

This simple test illustrates the most convincing reason for using active and interactive learning with young people: People learn best through experience. Or to put it even more simply, people learn by doing.

Learning by doing is what active learning is all about. No more sitting quietly in chairs and listening to a speaker expound theories about God—that's passive learning. Active learning gets kids out of their chairs and into the experience of life. With active learning, kids get to *do* what they're studying. They *feel* the effects of the principles you teach. They *learn* by experiencing truth firsthand.

Active learning works because it recognizes three basic learning needs and uses them in concert to enable young people to make discoveries on their own and to find practical life applications for the truths they believe.

So what are these three basic learning needs?
1. Teenagers need action.
2. Teenagers need to think.
3. Teenagers need to talk.

Read on to find out exactly how these needs will be met by using the active and interactive learning techniques in Group's Core Belief Bible Study Series in your youth group.

1. Teenagers Need Action

Aircraft pilots know well the difference between passive and active learning. Their passive learning comes through listening to flight instructors and reading flight-instruction books. Their active learning comes through actually flying an airplane or flight simulator. Books and lectures may be helpful, but pilots really learn to fly by manipulating a plane's controls themselves.

We can help young people learn in a similar way. Though we may engage students passively in some reading and listening to teachers, their understanding and application of God's Word will really take off through simulated and real-life experiences.

Forms of active learning include simulation games; role-plays; service projects; experiments; research projects; group pantomimes; mock trials; construction projects; purposeful games; field trips; and, of course, the most powerful form of active learning—real-life experiences.

We can more fully explain active learning by exploring four of its characteristics:

● **Active learning is an adventure.** Passive learning is almost always predictable. Students sit passively while the teacher or speaker follows a planned outline or script.

In active learning, kids may learn lessons the teacher never envisioned. Because the leader trusts students to help create the learning experience, learners may venture into unforeseen discoveries. And often the teacher learns as much as the students.

● **Active learning is fun and captivating.** What are we communicating when we say, "OK, the fun's over—time to talk about God"? What's the hidden message? That joy is separate from God? And that learning is separate from joy?

What a shame.

Active learning is not joyless. One seventh-grader we interviewed clearly remembered her best Sunday school lesson: "Jesus was the light, and we went into a dark room and shut off the lights. We had a candle, and we learned that Jesus is the light and the dark can't shut off the light." That's active learning. Deena enjoyed the lesson. She had fun. And she learned.

Active learning intrigues people. Whether they find a foot-washing experience captivating or maybe a bit uncomfortable, they learn. And they learn on a level deeper than any work sheet or teacher's lecture could ever reach.

● **Active learning involves everyone.** Here the difference between passive and active learning becomes abundantly clear. It's like the difference between watching a football game on television and actually playing in the game.

The "trust walk" provides a good example of involving everyone in active learning. Half of the group members put on blindfolds; the other half serve as guides. The "blind" people trust the guides to lead them through the building or outdoors. The guides prevent the blind people from falling down stairs or tripping over rocks. Everyone needs to participate to learn the inherent lessons of trust, faith, doubt, fear, confidence, and servanthood. Passive spectators of this experience would learn little, but participants learn a great deal.

● **Active learning is focused through debriefing.** Activity simply for activity's sake doesn't usually result in good learning. Debriefing—evaluating an experience by discussing it in pairs or small groups—helps focus the experience and draw out its meaning. Debriefing helps sort and order the information students gather during the experience. It helps learners relate the recently experienced activity to their lives.

The process of debriefing is best started immediately after an experience. We use a three-step process in debriefing: reflection, interpretation, and application.

Reflection—This first step asks the students, "How did you feel?" Active-learning experiences typically evoke an emotional reaction, so it's appropriate to begin debriefing at that level.

Some people ask, "What do feelings have to do with education?" Feelings have everything to do with education. Think back again to that time in your life when you learned a big lesson. In all likelihood, strong feelings accompanied that lesson. Our emotions tend to cement things into our memories.

When you're debriefing, use open-ended questions to probe feelings. Avoid questions that can be answered with a "yes" or "no." Let your learners know that there are no wrong answers to these "feeling" questions. Everyone's feelings are valid.

Interpretation—The next step in the debriefing process asks, "What does this mean to you? How is this experience like or unlike some other aspect of your life?" Now you're asking people to identify a message or principle from the experience.

You want your learners to discover the message for themselves. So instead of telling students your answers, take the time to ask questions that encourage self-discovery. Use Scripture and discussion in pairs or small groups to explore how the actions and effects of the activity might translate to their lives.

Alert! Some of your people may interpret wonderful messages that you never intended. That's not failure! That's the Holy Spirit at work. God allows us to catch different glimpses of his kingdom even when we all look through the same glass.

Application—The final debriefing step asks, "What will you do about it?" This step moves learning into action. Your young people have shared a common experience. They've discovered a principle. Now they must create something new with what they've just experienced and interpreted. They must integrate the message into their lives.

The application stage of debriefing calls for a decision. Ask your students how they'll change, how they'll grow, what they'll do as a result of your time together.

2. Teenagers Need to Think

Today's students have been trained not to think. They aren't dumber than previous generations. We've simply conditioned them not to use their heads.

You see, we've trained our kids to respond with the simplistic answers they think the teacher wants to hear. Fill-in-the-blank student workbooks and teachers who ask dead-end questions such as "What's the capital of Delaware?" have produced kids and adults who have learned not to think.

And it doesn't just happen in junior high or high school. Our children are schooled very early not to think. Teachers attempt to help kids read with nonsensical fill-in-the-blank drills, word scrambles, and missing-letter puzzles.

Helping teenagers think requires a paradigm shift in how we teach. We need to plan for and set aside time for higher-order thinking and be willing to reduce our time spent on lower-order parroting. Group's Core Belief Bible Study Series is designed to help you do just that.

Thinking classrooms look quite different from traditional classrooms. In most church environments, the teacher does most of the talking and hopes that knowledge will transmit from his or her brain to the students'. In thinking settings, the teacher coaches students to ponder, wonder, imagine, and problem-solve.

3. Teenagers Need to Talk

Everyone knows that the person who learns the most in any class is the teacher. Explaining a concept to someone else is usually more helpful to the explainer than to the listener. So why not let the students do more teaching? That's one of the chief benefits of letting kids do the talking. This process is called interactive learning.

What is interactive learning? Interactive learning occurs when students discuss and work cooperatively in pairs or small groups.

Interactive learning encourages learners to work together. It honors the fact that students can learn from one another, not just from the teacher. Students work together in pairs or small groups to accomplish shared goals. They build together, discuss together, and present together. They teach each other and learn from one another. Success as a group is celebrated. Positive interdependence promotes individual and group learning.

Interactive learning not only helps people learn but also helps learners feel better about themselves and get along better with others. It accomplishes these things more effectively than the independent or competitive methods.

Here's a selection of interactive learning techniques that are used in Group's Core Belief Bible Study Series. With any of these models, leaders may assign students to specific partners or small groups. This will maximize cooperation and learning by preventing all the "rowdies" from linking up. And it will allow for new friendships to form outside of established cliques.

Following any period of partner or small-group work, the leader may reconvene the entire class for large-group processing. During this time the teacher may ask for reports or discoveries from individuals or teams. This technique builds in accountability for the teacherless pairs and small groups.

Pair-Share—With this technique each student turns to a partner and responds to a question or problem from the teacher or leader. Every learner responds. There are no passive observers. The teacher may then ask people to share their partners' responses.

Study Partners—Most curricula and most teachers call for Scripture passages to be read to the whole class by one person. One reads; the others doze.

Why not relinquish some teacher control and let partners read and react with each other? They'll all be involved—and will learn more.

Learning Groups—Students work together in small groups to create a model, design artwork, or study a passage or story; then they discuss what they learned through the experience. Each person in the learning group may be assigned a specific role. Here are some examples:

Reader

Recorder (makes notes of key thoughts expressed during the reading or discussion)

Checker (makes sure everyone understands and agrees with answers arrived at by the group)

Encourager (urges silent members to share their thoughts)

When everyone has a specific responsibility, knows what it is, and contributes to a small group, much is accomplished and much is learned.

Summary Partners—One student reads a paragraph, then the partner summarizes the paragraph or interprets its meaning. Partners alternate roles with each paragraph.

The paraphrasing technique also works well in discussions. Anyone who wishes to share a thought must first paraphrase what the previous person said. This sharpens listening skills and demonstrates the power of feedback communication.

Jigsaw—Each person in a small group examines a different concept, Scripture, or part of an issue. Then each teaches the others in the group. Thus, all members teach, and all must learn the others' discoveries. This technique is called a jigsaw because individuals are responsible to their group for different pieces of the puzzle.

JIGSAW EXAMPLE

Here's an example of a jigsaw.

Assign four-person teams. Have teammates each number off from one to four. Have all the Ones go to one corner of the room, all the Twos to another corner, and so on.

Tell team members they're responsible for learning information in their numbered corners and then for teaching their team members when they return to their original teams.

Give the following assignments to various groups:

Ones: Read Psalm 22. Discuss and list the prophecies made about Jesus.

Twos: Read Isaiah 52:13–53:12. Discuss and list the prophecies made about Jesus.

Threes: Read Matthew 27:1-32. Discuss and list the things that happened to Jesus.

Fours: Read Matthew 27:33-66. Discuss and list the things that happened to Jesus.

After the corner groups meet and discuss, instruct all learners to return to their original teams and report what they've learned. Then have each team determine which prophecies about Jesus were fulfilled in the passages from Matthew.

Call on various individuals in each team to report one or two prophecies that were fulfilled.

You Can Do It Too!

All this information may sound revolutionary to you, but it's really not. God has been using active and interactive learning to teach his people for generations. Just look at Abraham and Isaac, Jacob and Esau, Moses and the Israelites, Ruth and Boaz. And then there's Jesus, who used active learning all the time!

Group's Core Belief Bible Study Series makes it easy for you to use active and interactive learning with your group. The active and interactive elements are automatically built in! Just follow the outlines, and watch as your kids grow through experience and positive interaction with others.

FOR DEEPER STUDY

For more information on incorporating active and interactive learning into your work with teenagers, check out these resources:

● *Why Nobody Learns Much of Anything at Church: And How to Fix It*, by Thom and Joani Schultz (Group Publishing) and

● *Do It! Active Learning in Youth Ministry*, by Thom and Joani Schultz (Group Publishing).

your evaluation of

core belief

Bible Study Series
for junior high/middle school

the truth about
EVIL

Group Publishing, Inc.
Attention: Core Belief Talk-Back
P.O. Box 481
Loveland, CO 80539
Fax: (970) 679-4370

Please help us continue to provide innovative and useful resources for ministry. After you've led the studies in this volume, take a moment to fill out this evaluation; then mail or fax it to us at the address above. Thanks!

● ● ● ● ● ●

1. As a whole, this book has been (circle one)

not very helpful   very helpful
1   2   3   4   5   6   7   8   9   10

2. The best things about this book:

3. How this book could be improved:

4. What I will change because of this book:

5. Would you be interested in field-testing future Core Belief Bible Studies and giving us your feedback? If so, please complete the information below:

Name _____

Street address _____

City _____ State _____ Zip _____

Daytime telephone (____) _____ Date _____

THANKS!